To

_____

From

_____

Spirit of a Champion
Copyright ©1998 by Jay Carty
Copyright ©2002 DaySpring Cards, Inc.
Published by Garborg's™ a brand of DaySpring Cards, Inc.
Siloam Springs, Arkansas

Design by Hot Dish Advertising

Scripture quotations are from the following sources: THE HOLY BIBLE, NEW INTERNATIONAL VERSION® NIV® ©1973, 1978, 1984 by International Bible Society. Used by permission of Zondervan Publishing House. The Holy Bible, New Century Version (NCV) ©1987, 1988, 1991 by Word Publishing, Dallas, Texas 75039. Used by permission. THE MESSAGE © Eugene H. Peterson 1993, 1994, 1995. Used by permission of NavPress Publishing Group. All rights reserved. The Living Bible (TLB) ©1971 by permission of Tyndale House Publishers, Inc., Wheaton, IL. Holy Bible, New Living Translation (NLT) ©1996 by permission of Tyndale House Publishers, Inc., Wheaton, IL.

ISBN 1-58061-499-X

As simple as it sounds, we all must try to be the best person we can: by making the best choices, by making the most of the talents we've been given.

MARY LOU RETTON,
GYMNAST, OLYMPIC GOLD MEDALIST

January 1

Even though I may be winning Olympic medals,
I believe my finest day is yet unknown—that won't be
until I stand with Jesus and He's showing me all the
things that I trust Him for now by faith.

DAVE JOHNSON, DECATHLETE, OLYMPIC BRONZE MEDALIST

December 31

Courage is not the absence of fear, but simply

moving on with dignity despite that fear.

PAT RILEY, NBA COACH

January 2

I have fought the good fight, I have finished the race, I have kept the faith. Now there is in store for me the crown of righteousness, which the Lord, the righteous Judge, will award to me on that day—and not only to me, but also to all who have longed for his appearing.

2 TIMOTHY 4:7-8 NIV

December 30

I've learned that you've got to give everything over to the Lord, and that no matter what you do in life, you can be used of God.

EUGENE ROBINSON, NFL SAFETY

January 3

I tell myself to enjoy my swimming, to have fun with interviews, and to get the most out of being young. On the starting blocks before my first Olympic race, I was smiling because I was having fun. That's what it is all about—having fun.

JANET EVANS, SWIMMER,
THREE-TIME OLYMPIC GOLD MEDALIST

December 29

I enjoy winning, but there are benefits in losing, too.

Before you can be a winner, you have to learn to lose.

ISAIAH THOMAS, NBA GUARD

January 4

Do not let what you cannot do interfere with
what you can do.

JOHN WOODEN, COLLEGE BASKETBALL COACH

December 28

Do you not know that in a race all the runners run,

but only one gets the prize? Run in such

a way as to get the prize.

1 CORINTHIANS 9:24 NIV

January 5

God's trying to give you guidelines and teach you the right ways to do things. Whether you're rich or poor, successful or not successful, what's in that Book is the way to do things.

JEFF GORDON, NASCAR RACE DRIVER

December 27

Practice does not make the athlete. It is the quality and intensity of practice that makes the athlete, not just repeated practicing.

Ray Meyer, College Basketball Coach

January 6

In baseball success is very elusive, considering that the greatest hitters of all time only got a hit 3 to 4 out of every 10 at-bats. That means that they actually failed 6 to 7 times out of 10. If any of the great hitters had taken time to think about how many times they had failed, they never would have been successful.

DOUG JONES, MAJOR LEAGUE PITCHER

December 26

When I seem to have no one to turn to,

God is always there.

DANTE BICHETTE, MAJOR LEAGUE HITTER

January 7

Glory to God in the highest, and on earth peace

to men on whom his favor rests.

LUKE 2:14 NIV

December 25

Class is striving hard to be the best at what you do, while taking the needs of others into consideration.

ROGER STAUBACH, NFL QUARTERBACK

January 8

One reason why I think a great deal of Jesus is because He never pointed out the weaknesses of people and never dwelt on their failures and shortcomings. He always thought of the dream that God had for their lives.

BOB RICHARDS, POLE VAULTER,
TWO-TIME OLYMPIC GOLD MEDALIST

December 24

Discipline is the whole key to being successful.

We all get 24 hours each day. That's the only fair thing;

it's the only thing that's equal. What we do with those

24 hours is up to us.

SAM HUFF, NFL LINEBACKER

January 9

I want to spend my time wisely. That means spending much of it with my wife and children, growing together, learning together, making life interesting for one another.

MIKE SINGLETARY, NFL LINEBACKER

December 23

They that wait upon the Lord shall renew their strength; they shall mount up with wings as eagles; they shall run and not be weary; and they shall walk, and not faint.

ISAIAH 40:31 KJV

January 10

In baseball terms, the middle-relief man may not be as important as the closer or starter, but in the game of life I can play just as important a role doing that as I could doing anything else. That's the role God has given me and I can be content with that.

BILL SAMPEN, MAJOR LEAGUE PITCHER

December 22

Sometimes when I'm on tour...it's difficult with no one to talk to or no one who understands. But there's always the Lord who's with me and will help me to strengthen myself and be strong in Him.

MICHAEL CHANG, PROFESSIONAL TENNIS PLAYER

January 11

Class is being honest—both with others and with yourself. Class is treating others as you would like them to treat you.

JACK NICKLAUS, PROFESSIONAL GOLFER

December 21

I prepared myself beforehand until I knew that I could

do what I had to do. Then I had faith.

JOE NAMATH, NFL QUARTERBACK

January 12

The heavens tell of the glory of God.... The sun lives in the heavens where God placed it. It bursts forth like a radiant bridegroom after his wedding. It rejoices like a great athlete eager to run the race.

PSALM 19:1,4-5 NLT

December 20

There's no substitute for guts.

PAUL "BEAR" BRYANT, COLLEGE FOOTBALL COACH

January 13

If I'm not being a role model for my own kids,

then I have no business being anybody else's

children's role model.

REGGIE WHITE, NFL DEFENSIVE TACKLE

December 19

To repeat successes of the past, follow your old program. Don't get fancy; just be consistent.

BILL RODGERS, DISTANCE RUNNER

January 14

Consistency is what counts; you have to be able to do things over and over again.

HANK AARON, MAJOR LEAGUE OUTFIELDER

December 18

If you give, you will get! Your gift will return to you in full and overflowing measure, pressed down, shaken together to make room for more, and running over. Whatever measure you use to give—large or small—will be used to measure what is given back to you.

LUKE 6:38 TLB

January 15

My faith in God has given me a strength that I was

searching for and never had.

JOHN VANBIESBROUCK, NHL GOALIE

December 17

I thought my dreams were over, but God works in mysterious ways. There's no way I could be here right now except through Him.

LAURA WILKINSON, DIVER, U.S. GOLD MEDALLIST

January 16

I watch players, all players. I watch them on television,

at college games, in the playground.

You can learn from anybody.

JULIUS ERVING, NBA FORWARD

December 16

A few mistakes don't worry me; what worries me is when you make mistakes and then forget your role on the team and start to worry about your ego.

DIGGER PHELPS, COLLEGE BASKETBALL COACH

January 17

The joy of the Lord is your strength.

NEHEMIAH 8:10 TLB

December 15

I stay after practice to catch passes. I look at myself as an encouragement to the [average] man who doesn't have great speed. I work hard. If you work hard too, you can make it.

STEVE LARGENT, NFL WIDE RECEIVER

January 18

You're never as good or as bad as they say you are. In the context of eternity, my football achievements mean very little. To a large extent, my job consists of running downfield, beating a guy, and catching a ball—no big deal. Nothing to worry about.

STEVE LARGENT, NFL WIDE RECEIVER

December 14

You've got to believe deep inside yourself that you're destined to do great things.

JOE PATERNO, COLLEGE FOOTBALL COACH

January 19

The difference between the possible and the impossible lies in the man's determination.

TOMMY LASORDA, MAJOR LEAGUE MANAGER

December 13

Pursue a righteous life—a life of wonder, faith, love, steadiness, courtesy. Run hard and fast in the faith. Seize the eternal life, the life you were called to.

1 TIMOTHY 6:11-12 THE MESSAGE

January 20

There are only two teams. You can play on God's team, or you can play against Him.

JOE GIBBS, NFL COACH

December 12

I was nervous, so I read the New Testament. I read the verse about having no fear, and I felt relaxed. Then I jumped farther than I ever jumped before in my life.

WILLYE WHITE, LONG JUMP, OLYMPIC SILVER MEDALIST

January 21

Every time I stepped on the field, I believed my team
was going to walk off the winner, somehow, some way.

ROGER STAUBACH, NFL QUARTERBACK

December 11

One man can be a crucial ingredient on a team,

but one man cannot make a team.

KAREEM ABDUL-JABBAR, NBA CENTER

January 22

God is our refuge and strength,

always ready to help in times of trouble.

So we will not fear.

PSALM 46:1-2 NLT

December 10

To gain success you need to be dedicated, have a sense

of balance in your life, and be willing to take a risk.

**BONNIE BLAIR, SPEEDSKATER,
FIVE-TIME OLYMPIC GOLD MEDALIST**

January 23

Faith is so important, but you don't know what faith is until it's been tested by the fire. My faith has been tested. The last impression I would want to give is I'm some kind of superhuman...who didn't go through down moments. But my driving force was the strength and peace and comfort I received through Christ.

DAVE DRAVECKY, MAJOR LEAGUE PITCHER

December 9

I don't like to think about injuries. I am just happy to be out there. I realize that I have been blessed with athletic ability, so I just try to enjoy myself every game because, after all, basketball is still just a game.

LARRY NANCE, NBA FORWARD

January 24

Many of my friends from home have been sent to jail for drugs. But I didn't want to end up like that. I would go to the gym every night to practice. Once the janitor said, "It's Saturday night. Why aren't you out at the parties like everybody else?" I said, "Parties won't take me where I want to go."

KEVIN JOHNSON, NBA GUARD

December 8

Open your mouth and taste, open your eyes and

see—how good God is. Blessed are you who run to him.

Worship God if you want the best; worship

opens doors to all his goodness.

PSALM 34:8-9 THE MESSAGE

January 25

You set a goal to be the best and then you work hard

every hour of every day, striving to reach that goal.

If you allow yourself to settle for anything less than

number one, you are cheating yourself.

DON SHULA, NFL COACH

December 7

I play like I'm eight feet tall.

DAWN STALEY, 5'6" ABL GUARD

January 26

I've always believed that the desire must come from within, not as a result of being driven by coaches or parents.

DAWN FRASER, SWIMMER,
THREE-TIME OLYMPIC GOLD MEDALIST

December 6

One night I asked the Lord to come into my life, and since that time, I have firmly believed that the Lord was...watching over me the day I crashed.

MICHAEL WALTRIP, RACE CAR DRIVER

January 27

Where can I go from your Spirit?... If I go up to the heavens, you are there; if I make my bed in the depths, you are there. If I rise on the wings of the dawn, if I settle on the far side of the sea, even there your hand will guide me, your right hand will hold me fast.

PSALM 139:7-10 NIV

December 5

Sometimes I find myself getting a little too serious.

When I'm having fun, it breaks the tension

and I play much better.

ANDRE AGASSI, PROFESSIONAL TENNIS PLAYER

January 28

I have the desire to do God's will. I try to work on my

spiritual condition on a daily basis.

JEFF MUSSELMAN, MAJOR LEAGUE PITCHER

December 4

As long as I can focus on enjoying what I'm doing, on having fun, I know I'll play well.

STEFFI GRAF, PROFESSIONAL TENNIS PLAYER

January 29

When things go bad, it's easy to point fingers.
People who attempt to switch the blame are afraid to
fail. We've all been afraid to fail before a game, but it
shouldn't stop us from continuing, and from doing
what we have to do to get the job done.

JOHN ELWAY, NFL QUARTERBACK

December 3

I press on toward the goal to win the prize for which

God has called me heavenward in Christ Jesus.

PHILIPPIANS 3:14 NIV

January 30

Most competitors are so focused they don't want to take time to say hello, but I'm always chatting. It relaxes me. When I run relaxed, I have fun, and no one can beat me.

FLORENCE GRIFFITH JOYNER, SPRINTER,
THREE-TIME OLYMPIC GOLD MEDALIST

December 2

It's not Super Bowl rings, but the crown of eternal life
Christ has won for us.

MIKE HOLMGREN, NFL COACH

January 31

Experience is a hard teacher because she gives the test first, the lesson afterward.

VERNON LAW, MAJOR LEAGUE PITCHER

December 1

I'm gifted, but I've worked for everything I've gotten.

Gordie Howe and Bobby Orr worked hard too.

Like them, I didn't say, "I'm gifted.

I don't have to work anymore"

WAYNE GRETZKY, NHL CENTER

February 1

As you know, we consider blessed those who have persevered.... The Lord is full of compassion and mercy.

JAMES 5:11 NIV

November 30

Coming down the stretch, I think about the same thing all the time. Put your head down and go as fast as you can—put winning or losing out of your mind—just concentrate on swimming as fast as you can.

JANET EVANS, SWIMMER,
THREE-TIME OLYMPIC GOLD MEDALIST

February 2

I don't have to go up to the guys and tell them to

hustle. They see the way I play.

Leadership comes by example.

WILLIE STARGELL, MAJOR LEAGUE FIRST BASEMAN

November 29

If you are honest with yourself and can look into a
mirror and believe that you have given 100 percent,
you should feel proud. If you cannot,
then there is more work to be done.

JOHN HAVLICEK, NBA FORWARD

February 3

Due to my size limitation, when I came into the NBA other players tried to test me right away. But once they saw I wasn't going to be tentative or intimidated, most of that stuff stopped. Now it's fun to go out there against the league's best, knowing that you have earned their respect through hard work and dedication.

MARK PRICE, NBA GUARD

November 28

The fruit of the righteous is a tree of life,

and he who wins souls is wise.

PROVERBS 11:30 NIV

February 4

Although competition is important, you must put it in perspective. If it's overemphasized, you lose a sense of what you're doing. You'll stop having fun.

BERNIE KOSAR, NFL QUARTERBACK

November 27

My faith's a rock.... It is my strength; it gives me inner peace. Without my faith, I'd be in real bad shape. Faith gives a man hope and hope is what life is all about.

TOM LANDRY, NFL COACH

February 5

We can't go back no matter how much we ache to do so. All we can do is give thanks for what was.... Then saying goodbye to those times and loved ones, we can put our hand in the hand of Him who gave orbit to the sun and the moon and the stars, and trust that He has a course for our lives as well.

DAVE DRAVECKY, MAJOR LEAGUE PITCHER

November 26

It's great to win, but it's also great fun just to be in the thick of any truly well- and hard-fought contest against opponents you respect, whatever the outcome.

JACK NICKLAUS, PROFESSIONAL GOLFER

February 6

Let your roots grow down into him and draw up nourishment from him. See that you go on growing in the Lord, and become strong and vigorous in the truth you were taught. Let your lives overflow with joy and thanksgiving for all he has done.

COLOSSIANS 2:7 TLB

November 25

Success is a peace of mind which is a direct result of...knowing that you did your best to become the best you are capable of becoming.

JOHN WOODEN, COLLEGE BASKETBALL COACH

February 7

I'd like my teammates to describe me as a man of

integrity—both on and off the field.

WALT WEISS, MAJOR LEAGUE SHORTSTOP

November 24

I've always played baseball because I love the game. So regardless of whether I hit a 440-foot home run or strike out, the game will always be fun. All I want is to be able to get in some quality cuts every at-bat.

BO JACKSON,
NFL RUNNING BACK AND MAJOR LEAGUE OUTFIELDER

February 8

I'm a firm believer in quiet confidence. By that I mean
knowing inwardly that you are good, and not exhibiting
a boastful attitude outwardly. If an athlete doesn't
believe in himself, no one else will.

DICK VAN ARSDALE, NBA FORWARD

November 23

Therefore, since we are surrounded by such a great cloud of witnesses, let us throw off everything that hinders and the sin that so easily entangles, and let us run with perseverance the race marked out for us.

Let us fix our eyes on Jesus, the author and perfecter of our faith.

HEBREWS 12:1-2 NIV

February 9

The Indy 500 is the biggest race in the world. You could come here for years and never win and still enjoy yourself. The competition here alone makes it worth it.

EMERSON FITTIPALDI, RACE CAR DRIVER

November 22

Doing anything well doesn't just lead to success—
it is success. Real success in life begins with
acceptance—acceptance of God's love for you
as a unique and special person.

KYLE ROTE, JR., PROFESSIONAL SOCCER PLAYER

February 10

My perception of God was of someone unreachable,

but I found that He is a very personal God.

JEFF MUSSELMAN, MAJOR LEAGUE PITCHER

November 21

Have fun doing whatever it is that you desire to accomplish. Learn it one step at a time, emphasizing the fundamentals, and do it because you love it, not because it's work.

PAUL WESTPHAL, NBA COACH

February 11

Βut thanks be to God! He gives us the victory

through our Lord Jesus Christ.

1 Corinthians 15:57 niv

November 20

Even though circumstances may cause interruptions and delays, never lose sight of your goal. Instead, prepare yourself in every way you can by increasing your knowledge and adding to your experience, so that you can make the most of opportunity when it occurs.

MARIO ANDRETTI, RACE CAR DRIVER

February 12

It's easy to get wrapped up in it all, but you've got to keep priorities. The first thing is family. I do nothing to jeopardize that.

JOHN WETTELAND, MAJOR LEAGUE PITCHER

November 19

A champion is someone who is bending over to exhaustion when no one else is watching.

MIA HAMM, PROFESSIONAL SOCCER PLAYER

February 13

Learn to compartmentalize yourself. You're an athlete for only a few more years. You have to live 80 or 90 years, so you had better find more things to do.

TOM SANDERS, NBA PLAYER

November 18

Love knows no limit to its endurance, no end to its

trust, no fading of its hope; it can outlast anything.

Love never fails.

1 CORINTHIANS 13:7-8 PHILLIPS

February 14

I think the most rewarding thing that can happen to a person is to find out God's purpose for him and go ahead and do it well.... Baseball is what God gave me—it's my purpose in life.

MIKE SCHMIDT, MAJOR LEAGUE THIRD BASEMAN

November 17

It's not the size of the dog in the fight,

but the size of the fight in the dog.

ARCHIE GRIFFEN,
TWO-TIME HEISMAN AWARD WINNER

February 15

It's important to keep all things in life in perspective.

Football is a game. Playing games is fun.

I never want to lose sight of that.

TROY AIKMAN, NFL QUARTERBACK

November 16

My definition of discipline is as follows: (1) Do what has to be done, when it has to be done, as well as it can be done, and (2) Do it that way all the time.

BOBBY KNIGHT, COLLEGE BASKETBALL COACH

February 16

Let me see your kindness to me in the morning,

for I am trusting you. Show me where to walk,

for my prayer is sincere.

PSALM 143:8 TLB

November 15

The most important thing in becoming a success is the three P's—practice, perseverance, and prayer.

DOAK WALKER, NFL RUNNING BACK

February 17

In the second grade, they asked us what we wanted to be. I said I wanted to be a ballplayer and they laughed. In the eighth grade, they asked us the same question. I said, "A ballplayer," and they laughed a little more. By the eleventh grade, no one was laughing.

JOHNNY BENCH, MAJOR LEAGUE CATCHER

November 14

It's amazing how much can be accomplished if no one cares who gets the credit.

BLANTON COLLIER, NFL COACH

February 18

The medals aren't the important thing.

The glory is nice but it doesn't last. It's all about

performing well and feeling deeply about it.

DALEY THOMPSON, DECATHLETE,
TWO-TIME OLYMPIC GOLD MEDALIST

November 13

Do you want to stand out? Then step down.
Be a servant. If you puff yourself up, you'll get the
wind knocked out of you. But if you're content to
simply be yourself, your life will count for plenty.

MATTHEW 23:11-12 THE MESSAGE

February 19

Leave as little to chance as possible.

Preparation is the key to success.

PAUL BROWN, NFL COACH

November 12

I use the word hungry to describe what I mean when I talk about desire. Being hungry provides you with the physical and mental energies necessary for success. The sacrifices that are necessary become easier when one places a goal or objective at a high level.

ARA PARSEGHIAN, COLLEGE FOOTBALL COACH

February 20

Specialists can never practice their specialties too much.

The danger is in not practicing enough.

Make that mistake, and soon you may not be in the

specialty business anymore.

JOHNNY UNITAS, NFL QUARTERBACK

November 11

A person needs a spiritual side to be complete.

SHANE BATTIER, NBA FORWARD

February 21

Be strong and take heart,

all you who hope in the Lord.

PSALM 31:24 NIV

November 10

Every single meet when they say, "On your mark," that feeling in my stomach and my throat, it's like the first time I ever ran. I always think, Why am I doing this? It's so nerve-racking. I can't sleep the night before. And as soon as the race is over I can't wait to do it again. Running is like a test of will.

Aimee Mullins, double amputee, Long Jump and Sprint Record Holder, Paralympics

February 22

I's basically taken all of me to get here—physically, mentally, and especially spiritually. You can't leave any one of those elements out to make it at this level.

JENNIFER AZZI, WNBA GUARD

November 9

Working together is fun. Winning is fun.

Just playing is fun.

JOE DUMARS, NBA GUARD

February 23

Make sure that the career you choose is one you enjoy. If you don't enjoy what you are doing, it will be difficult to give the extra time, effort, and devotion it takes to be a success. If it is a career that you find fun and enjoyable, then you will do whatever it takes.

KATHY WHITWORTH, PROFESSIONAL GOLFER

November 8

He has told you what he wants, and this is all it is:

to be fair and just and merciful, and to walk

humbly with your God.

MICAH 6:8 TLB

February 24

When I was a small boy in Kansas, a friend and I...talked about what we wanted to do when we grew up. I told him that I wanted to be a real major league baseball player, a genuine professional like Honus Wagner. My friend said that he'd like to be president of the United States. Neither of us got our wish.

DWIGHT D. EISENHOWER,
34TH PRESIDENT OF THE UNITED STATES

November 7

I't's not necessarily the amount of time you spend at practice that counts; it's what you put into the practice.

ERIC LINDROS, NHL CENTER

February 25

Desire and determination must

overcome disappointment.

WALTER ALSTON, MAJOR LEAGUE MANAGER

November 6

I am aware of how crucial it is for kids with Tourette to have a role model. Until there is a cure, I will always suffer some symptoms. But I believe God will never give me more than I can handle.

JIM EISENREICH, MAJOR LEAGUE OUTFIELDER

February 26

Trust steadily in God, hope unswervingly, love extravagantly. And the best of the three is love.

1 CORINTHIANS 13:13 THE MESSAGE

November 5

Success is not the result of spontaneous combustion.

You must set yourself on fire.

FRED SHERO, NHL COACH

February 27

Don't be good, be great. Strive to be exceptional.
Picture yourself making the great play. Picture yourself
making the great tackle. Don't let anyone stop you.

DAN HAMPTON, NFL DEFENSIVE LINEMAN

November 4

I only play well when I'm prepared.

If I don't practice the way I should, then I won't play

the way that I know I can.

IVAN LENDL, PROFESSIONAL TENNIS PLAYER

February 28

How can you say you love somebody, if an incident would cause you to stop loving them? The love that the Lord wants us to have for people does not change if they wrong us or if something else happens. You still love them. I made a choice to love him regardless of what happened.

EVANDER HOLYFIELD, PROFESSIONAL BOXER,
(SPEAKING OF MIKE TYSON)

November 3

For the Lord gives wisdom, and from his mouth come knowledge and understanding. He holds victory in store for the upright, he is a shield to those whose walk is blameless, for he guards the course of the just and protects the way of his faithful ones.

PROVERBS 2:6-8 NIV

February 29

You shouldn't worry about the fans or the press or trying to satisfy the expectations of anyone else. All that matters is whether you [can] look in the mirror and honestly tell the person you see there that you've done your best.

JOHN MCKAY, NFL COACH

November 2

After searching for the meaning of life for over ten
years, I found the meaning in Jesus Christ.

JULIUS ERVING, NBA FORWARD

March 1

D̲on't be afraid to fail. Experience is just mistakes

you won't make anymore.

J̲OE G̲ARAGIOLA, M̲AJOR L̲EAGUE C̲ATCHER

November 1

It's not so much what you go through, it's how you handle the bad night, a bad season, or a hard lesson you get in the playoffs. That's what makes not just great players but champions.

AVERY JOHNSON, NBA GUARD

March 2

Your word is a lamp to my feet

and a light for my path.

PSALM 119:105 NIV

October 31

Be more concerned with your character than your reputation, because your character is what you really are, while your reputation is merely what others think you are.

JOHN WOODEN, COLLEGE BASKETBALL COACH

March 3

Have you ever had a day when you get up in the morning and something goes wrong and you say, "Jiminy, it's going to be one of those days"? I bet you do that a lot; I've done it. But you know what I say now? "Well, it started out bad, but it's still going to be a great day." You'd be amazed how doing that turns a bad day into a good day.

GERRY FAUST, COLLEGE FOOTBALL COACH

October 30

The best description of class I can give you is not an original but comes from a famous work by Kipling. Entering the Centre Court at Wimbledon, as you look up, you see these words: "If you can meet with triumph and disaster and treat those two impostors just the same, if you can do that, you will have class."

JOHN NEWCOMBE, PROFESSIONAL TENNIS PLAYER

March 4

Most people assume you change with success. Not me.
I believe you have to remember where you started to
completely understand what you have accomplished.

TROY AIKMAN, NFL QUARTERBACK

October 29

Blessed are all who fear the Lord, who walk in his ways. You will eat the fruit of your labor; blessings and prosperity will be yours.

PSALM 128:1-2 NIV

March 5

I want to make sure I take advantage of the

opportunity I have to represent [God].

HUBERT DAVIS, NBA GUARD

October 28

Individual commitment to a group effort—that is
what makes a team work, a company work, a society
work, a civilization work.

VINCE LOMBARDI, NFL COACH

March 6

Failure does not come from losing, but from not trying.

LARRY BROWN, NBA COACH

October 27

I've always believed that anybody with a little ability,

a little guts, and the desire to apply himself can make it.

He can make anything he wants to make of himself.

WILLIE SHOEMAKER, PROFESSIONAL JOCKEY

March 7

My flesh and my heart may fail, but God is the

strength of my heart and my portion forever.

PSALM 73:26 NIV

October 26

The most important thing is to love your sport. Never do it to please someone else—the desire has to be yours. That is all that will justify the hard work needed to achieve success. Compete against yourself, not others, for you are truly your best competition.

PEGGY FLEMING, FIGURE SKATER, OLYMPIC GOLD MEDALIST

March 8

I now know that it is more important to care what God thinks than what people think.

DOUG PELFREY, NFL PLACE KICKER

October 25

Some basic principles that I've found important to find fulfillment in whatever you do are: Love God, yourself, and others, in that order. Set your priorities and work toward them with consistency, faith, and self-discipline.

JANET LYNN SALOMON, FIGURE SKATER

March 9

Sport is only sport if the results are unpredictable.

Otherwise, we would gain the same entertainment by

watching the Harlem Globetrotters.

SIR ARTHUR GOLD, CHAIRMAN,
BRITISH OLYMPIC ASSOCIATION

October 24

Walk with me and work with me—watch how I do it.

Learn the unforced rhythms of grace. I won't lay

anything heavy or ill-fitting on you. Keep company with

me and you'll learn to live freely and lightly.

MATTHEW 11:29–30 THE MESSAGE

March 10

Confidence comes from hours and days and weeks and years of constant work and dedication. When I'm in the last two minutes of a December playoff game, I'm drawing confidence from wind sprints I did the previous March.

ROGER STAUBACH, NFL QUARTERBACK

October 23

Being involved in competition is a privilege and an opportunity. Seek to make the most of that opportunity by pushing yourself to the limit of your abilities. When it is over, you will have earned the respect of your opponents, your coaches, and yourself.

TONY LaRUSSA, MAJOR LEAGUE MANAGER

March 11

You're never as good as everyone tells you when you win, and you're never as bad as they say when you lose.

LOU HOLTZ, COLLEGE FOOTBALL COACH

October 22

Concentration is the ability to think about absolutely

nothing when it is absolutely necessary.

RAY KNIGHT, PROFESSIONAL BASEBALL COACH

March 12

M<small>OST</small> of all, let love guide your life.

C<small>OLOSSIANS</small> 3:14 <small>TLB</small>

October 21

Setting a goal is not the main thing. It is deciding how you will go about achieving it and staying with that plan. The key is discipline. Without it, there is no morale.

TOM LANDRY, NFL COACH

March 13

There is one key point [to remember] in picking the

so-called "great athlete." He must perform

with the team in mind.

JOHN MADDEN, NFL COACH

October 20

If you are under 18 years old, you have only lived about one-fourth of your life. That means you have the remaining three-fourths of your life to accomplish anything you want. Don't blow it. Don't do drugs. If you are doing them, stop it. Get some help. If you haven't experimented with drugs, don't start. Give yourself a chance to succeed and be all the wonderful things you can be.

MICHAEL JORDAN, NBA GUARD

March 14

Jesus was the bravest, toughest man who ever walked

on the face of this earth.

REGGIE WHITE, NFL LINEMAN

October 19

I pray that you may enjoy good health and that all

may go well with you, even as your soul

is getting along well.

3 JOHN 1:2 NIV

March 15

My only feeling about superstition is that it's unlucky

to be behind at the end of a game.

BILL RUSSELL, NBA CENTER

October 18

They clutch and grab, and some teams play dirty, but it's the challenge that keeps you going. I love playing the game. It's no different than little kids who go out and play for the fun of it. We're just big kids playing a game. I love playing and I enjoy the thrill of competing.

WAYNE GRETZKY, NHL CENTER

March 16

You're good; you know it, but you don't wear it on
your sleeve. You don't have to tell anyone; they know it.
You start to tell them and it usually ends up
[being] lip service.

JOE GARAGIOLA, MAJOR LEAGUE CATCHER

October 17

Even [knowing I would] lose, I think I'd still compete.... It fulfills me to be able to compete. I never worry about winning or losing because when you compete, you are already a winner.

DALEY THOMPSON, DECATHLETE,
TWO-TIME OLYMPIC GOLD MEDALIST

March 17

A cheerful disposition is good for your health.

PROVERBS 17:22 THE MESSAGE

October 16

Football was the most important thing in my world.
It was my god and I was losing the ability to handle it.
I had to do a lot of thinking, but finally I gave
everything to God. He's given it back to me tenfold.

STEVE BARTKOWSKI, NFL QUARTERBACK

March 18

If things don't go your way, what can you do?
You cannot control the outcome. All you control is
your effort. If you worry too much about the results,
then your effort will suffer.

GEORGE BELL, MAJOR LEAGUE OUTFIELDER

October 15

If you can react the same way to winning and losing, that's a big accomplishment. That quality is important because it stays with you the rest of your life, and there's going to be a life after tennis that's a lot longer than your tennis life.

CHRIS EVERT, PROFESSIONAL TENNIS PLAYER

March 19

I've learned it's not always the most talented people

who make it, but those who don't give up.

ADAM BURT, NHL DEFENSEMAN

October 14

Take your everyday, ordinary life—your sleeping,

eating, going-to-work, and walking-around life—and

place it before God as an offering. Embracing what God

does for you is the best thing you can do for him.

ROMANS 12:1 THE MESSAGE

March 20

I pray often and I know God hears all my prayers. He may not answer them in the way I desire, but He knows what is best for me. I say a prayer before each game that I pitch. It is not a prayer for victory; it is a prayer of gratitude for my health and a plea for God's continued blessings.

RON GUIDRY, MAJOR LEAGUE PITCHER

October 13

We need people who influence their peers and who cannot be detoured from their convictions by peers who do not have the courage to have any convictions.

JOE PATERNO, COLLEGE FOOTBALL COACH

March 21

Ingenuity, plus courage, plus work, equals miracles.

BOB RICHARDS, POLE VAULTER,
TWO-TIME OLYMPIC GOLD MEDALIST

October 12

God calls me to be truthful,

to be frank and to step out in faith.

CHRIS CARTER, NFL WIDE RECEIVER

March 22

Whenever trouble comes your way, let it be an opportunity for joy. For when your faith is tested, your endurance has a chance to grow. So let it grow, for when your endurance is fully developed, you will be strong in character and ready for anything.

JAMES 1:2-4 NLT

October 11

Don't ever allow the pressure of competition to
be greater than the pleasure of competition.

JIM RODGERS, NBA COACH

March 23

I worked hard to learn to play first base. In the beginning, I used to make one terrible play a game. Then, I got so I'd make one a week, and finally, I'd pull a real bad one maybe once a month. At the end, I was trying to keep it down to one a season.

LOU GEHRIG, MAJOR LEAGUE FIRST BASEMAN

October 10

Your goal should be out of reach but not out of sight.

ANITA DeFRANTZ,
ROWING, OLYMPIC BRONZE MEDALIST

March 24

My contentment isn't based on where I stand on the money list. It isn't based on performance.

It is just based on Jesus Christ and having a right relationship with Him.

Scott Simpson, Professional Golfer

October 9

Let not the wise man boast of his wisdom or the strong man boast of his strength or the rich man boast of his riches, but let him who boasts boast about this: that he understands and knows me, that I am the Lord, who exercises kindness, justice and righteousness on earth, for in these I delight.

JEREMIAH 9:23-24 NIV

March 25

You have to expect things of yourself
before you can do them.

MICHAEL JORDAN, NBA GUARD

October 8

I just try to be the best I can be and hope
that is the best ever.

TIGER WOODS, GOLFER

March 26

I think guys watch you, and they respect the fact that

you compete hard and you're mentally tough.

Off the course, though, you can be sensitive

and kind and compassionate.

TOM LEHMAN, PROFESSIONAL GOLFER

October 7

If you read the Bible, you'll find out that a lot of things that deal with life, money, and everything are in there.

JEFF GORDON, NASCAR RACE DRIVER

March 27

Be strong! Be courageous! Don't be afraid of them!

For the Lord your God will be with you.

He will neither fail you nor forsake you.

DEUTERONOMY 31:6 TLB

October 6

I love to work. You've got to love what you do. It takes time, patience, long hours of work, trying to improve yourself every day.

JACK DEMPSEY, PROFESSIONAL BOXER

March 28

If we prepare thoughtfully, work hard, have faith in
God's plan for us, and are honest with ourselves,
we can live in peace with ourselves and
our accomplishments.

STAN SMITH, PROFESSIONAL TENNIS PLAYER

October 5

Part of being a champ is acting like a champ. You have to learn how to win and not run away when you lose. Everyone has bad stretches and real successes. Either way, you have to be careful not to lose your confidence or get too confident.

NANCY KERRIGAN, FIGURE SKATER, OLYMPIC SILVER MEDALIST

March 29

I want to change things. And I'm going to do my best to speak up about the things I think are wrong, whether it's in the university, in football, or in the country. The only way you can bring about a change is by doing something about it.

JOE PATERNO, COLLEGE FOOTBALL COACH

October 4

Whatever you do, whether in word or deed, do it

all in the name of the Lord Jesus, giving thanks

to God the Father through him.

COLOSSIANS 3:17 NIV

March 30

Be honest and work hard to get what you want. Don't take shortcuts; you only cheat yourself in the long run. Success is not measured by money or fame, but by how you feel about your own goals and accomplishments and the time and effort you put into them.

WILLIE STARGELL, MAJOR LEAGUE FIRST BASEMAN

October 3

Excellence is not a singular act but a habit.

You are what you do repeatedly.

SHAQUILLE O'NEAL, NBA CENTER

March 31

You cannot live a perfect day without doing something

for someone who will never be able to repay you.

SAM RUTIGLIANO, NFL COACH

October 2

I don't want my children to remember me as a great professional football player. I want them to remember me as a man of God.

REGGIE WHITE, NFL DEFENSIVE TACKLE

April 1

One thing God has spoken, two things have I heard:

that you, O God, are strong, and that you,

O Lord, are loving.

PSALM 62:11-12 NIV

October 1

You never fail until you stop trying.

FLORENCE GRIFFITH JOYNER, SPRINTER,
THREE-TIME OLYMPIC GOLD MEDALIST

April 2

I'm thankful for the ability God has given me. Without

Him I certainly wouldn't be where I am today.

People say I'm charismatic. Maybe it's because

I love this game and I don't mind showing it.

Playing ball is all I ever wanted to do.

KIRBY PUCKETT, MAJOR LEAGUE OUTFIELDER

September 30

D on't ever forget that you play with your soul

as well as your body.

KAREEM ABDUL-JABBAR, NBA CENTER

April 3

Young athletes, like all young people, must realize that
the future holds extraordinary challenges for everyone,
and they must accept those challenges as a part of life.

Honesty and integrity are most important.

Never compromise on what you know is right.

Lenny Wilkens, NBA Coach

September 29

Cling to wisdom—she will protect you. Love her—she will guard you. Getting wisdom is the most important thing you can do! And with your wisdom, develop common sense and good judgment.

PROVERBS 4:6-7 TLB

April 4

To win, you have to have talent and desire—

but desire is first.

SAM SNEAD, PROFESSIONAL GOLFER

September 28

To be a leader, you have to make people want to follow you, and nobody wants to follow someone who doesn't know where he's going.

JOE NAMATH, NFL QUARTERBACK

April 5

When I played sports, my parents never once said to me, "Did you win?" They'd say, "Did you have fun?" Winning the game was important, but not nearly as important as giving yourself a chance to win—playing as hard as you could and enjoying yourself.

JIM VALVANO, COLLEGE BASKETBALL COACH

September 27

You can pray all the time and I do. I'm not embarrassed to say that because I've been a praying man all my life. But nothing good comes without work.

EVANDER HOLYFIELD, PROFESSIONAL BOXER

April 6

Fear not, for I am with you. Do not be dismayed. I am your God. I will strengthen you; I will help you; I will uphold you with my victorious right hand.

ISAIAH 41:10 TLB

September 26

I approach hockey like a kid plays a game.
I'm much more interested in playing than in
contract talk. That's the flip side of athletes
that people rarely see.

MARIO LEMIEUX, NHL CENTER

April 7

I enjoy the thrill of competition and the excitement of

throwing the game-winning touchdown pass.

That's what makes this game so much fun. If you're not

having fun, then you're playing the wrong game.

DAN MARINO, NFL QUARTERBACK

September 25

If it had not been for the wind in my face,

I wouldn't be able to fly at all.

ARTHUR ASHE, PROFESSIONAL TENNIS PLAYER

April 8

You can never have too much fun.

GARY KNECHT,
COLLEGE FOOTBALL COACH

September 24

Who is wise and understanding among you?

Let him show it by his good life, by deeds done in the

humility that comes from wisdom.

JAMES 3:13 NIV

April 9

Although I still work hard every day to be the best

athlete I can possibly be, my ultimate confidence is in

God who created me and gives me the opportunity to

live and perform for Him.

RICO BROGNA, MAJOR LEAGUE FIRST BASEMAN

September 23

I'm always trying to give 100 percent to God—anything less would be unacceptable as far as Christ is concerned. He...gave 100 percent of Himself for us—He died for us! If He had given anything else we would fall well short of reaching God.

DAVE JOHNSON, DECATHLETE, OLYMPIC BRONZE MEDALIST

April 10

It only takes 10 seconds to mess up what you've been trying to build for a lifetime. Surround yourself with good people.

MIKE MARTIN, COLLEGE BASEBALL COACH

September 22

Every day is a new opportunity; you can build on yesterday's success or put its failures behind and start over again. That's the way life is.

With a new game every day.

BOB FELLER, MAJOR LEAGUE PITCHER

April 11

The Lord gives strength to his people;

the Lord blesses his people with peace.

PSALM 29:11 NIV

September 21

If you train hard, you'll not only be hard,

you'll be hard to beat.

HERSCHEL WALKER, NFL RUNNING BACK

April 12

Class is an intangible thing. Different people show it in different ways, but it does not take long to surface and it is easily recognizable.

ARTHUR J. ROONEY, NFL OWNER

September 20

I'm a firm believer in the theory that people only do their best at things they truly enjoy. It is difficult to excel at something you don't enjoy.

JACK NICKLAUS, PROFESSIONAL GOLFER

April 13

Sweat is the cologne of accomplishment.

HEYWOOD HALE BROUN, SPORTSWRITER

September 19

We ask God to give you a complete understanding of what he wants to do in your lives, and we ask him to make you wise with spiritual wisdom. Then the way you live will always honor and please the Lord, and you will continually do good, kind things for others. All the while, you will learn to know God better and better.

COLOSSIANS 1:9-10 NLT

April 14

As I became closer to God I realized I liked myself better when I was pleasing God than when I was pleasing my buddies.

ADAM BURT, NHL DEFENSEMAN

September 18

It doesn't do you any good to...get upset. If you lose, you should learn something from it. If it was your best pitch, well, you gave it your best shot.

If it wasn't, you shouldn't throw it again.

 OREL HERSHISER, MAJOR LEAGUE PITCHER

April 15

You hit home runs not by chance, but by preparation.

ROGER MARIS,
MAJOR LEAGUE OUTFIELDER

September 17

Scientists have proven that it's impossible to long-jump 30 feet, but I don't listen to that kind of talk. Thoughts like that have a way of sinking into your feet.

CARL LEWIS, SPRINTER/LONG JUMPER,
NINE-TIME OLYMPIC GOLD MEDALIST

April 16

I thank Christ Jesus our Lord, who has given me

strength, that he considered me faithful,

appointing me to his service.

1 TIMOTHY 1:12 NIV

September 16

Overall, a sound spiritual view of life, giving athletics

its proper place and perspective, is more important

than anything else.

DICK VAN ARSDALE, NBA FORWARD

April 17

Chance can allow you to accomplish a goal every once in a while, but consistent achievement happens only if you love what you are doing.

BART CONNER, GYMNAST,
TWO-TIME OLYMPIC GOLD MEDALIST

September 15

The mind is our most powerful muscle. If you think you're tired, you'll feel tired. I go out there thinking I'm going to complete every pass.

RON JAWORSKI, NFL QUARTERBACK

April 18

You have to set goals that are almost out of reach.
If you set a goal that is attainable without much work
or thought, you are stuck with something below your
true talent and potential.

STEVE GARVEY, MAJOR LEAGUE FIRST BASEMAN

September 14

Be content with who you are, and don't put on airs.

God's strong hand is on you; he'll promote you at the

right time. Live carefree before God;

he is most careful with you.

1 PETER 5:6-7 THE MESSAGE

April 19

Everything hasn't been easy or perfect but God has

been faithful and has never let me down.

JOHN KIDD, NFL PUNTER

September 13

If the human body recognized agony and frustration,

people would never run marathons, have babies,

or play baseball.

CARLTON FISK, MAJOR LEAGUE CATCHER

April 20

Success is never final. Failure is never fatal.

It's courage that counts.

SAM RUTIGLIANO, NFL COACH

September 12

We don't have to tell nobody at work that
we're saved. We show them.

DEION SANDERS, NFL DEFENSIVE LINEMAN

April 21

I am still confident of this: I will see the goodness of the Lord in the land of the living. Wait for the Lord; be strong and take heart and wait for the Lord.

PSALM 27:13-14 NIV

September 11

A winner is someone who recognizes his God given talents, works his tail off to develop them into skills, and uses these skills to accomplish his goals.

LARRY BIRD, NBA FORWARD

April 22

Temptation to experiment with various substances will always be there. You have to be above it. You have to be smarter. Smart enough to realize that it can only hurt you and your body. It takes guts to be a leader and not a follower. "Say no" and feel good about it and good about yourself.

CHARLES BARKLEY, NBA FORWARD

September 10

The answers to three questions will determine your success or failure. (1) Can people trust you to do your best? (2) Are you committed to the task at hand? (3) Do you care about other people and show it? If the answers to all these questions are yes, there is no way you can fail.

LOU HOLTZ, COLLEGE FOOTBALL COACH

April 23

God wants you to try your best. He wants you to give

glory for your achievements to Him. So obviously,

He wants you to win. It's still my job.

I still want to be the best I can be.

LOREN ROBERTS, PROFESSIONAL GOLFER

September 9

Blessed is the man who finds wisdom, the man who

gains understanding, for she is more profitable than

silver and yields better returns than gold.

PROVERBS 3:13-14 NIV

April 24

To me, there is a cycle in sports: "The more you enjoy it, the more you practice; the more you practice, the more you improve; therefore, you enjoy it more."

PANCHO GONZALEZ, PROFESSIONAL TENNIS PLAYER

September 8

When you have confidence, you can have a lot of fun, and when you have fun, you can do amazing things.

JOE NAMATH, NFL QUARTERBACK

April 25

When I start a play, I never know if I will be able to do what I would like. But I always go ahead and try. I have confidence in my ability as a basketball player. I guess deep down inside I know it will work.

JULIUS ERVING, NBA FORWARD

September 7

There is nothing in this world that can't be
accomplished through hard work and with the help
of God. Don't be afraid to talk to God.

After all, He is our Father.

JOHNNY UNITAS, NFL QUARTERBACK

April 26

The wisdom that comes from heaven is first of all

pure and full of quiet gentleness.

JAMES 3:17 TLB

September 6

If you don't invest very much, then defeat doesn't hurt

you very much and winning is not very exciting.

DICK VERMEIL, NFL COACH

April 27

I learned to fight. I worked and studied it. If I got beat up or did something sloppy in the gym, I'd go home and work on it until I got it right. It was hard work, but I didn't want to just be good. I wanted to be the best.

THOMAS HEARNS, PROFESSIONAL BOXER

September 5

Risking it all makes every moment meaningful;

the intensity is not something to fear or avoid,

but something to relish with a rowdy grin.

GLENN "DOC" RIVERS, NBA GUARD

April 28

If you don't stand for something,

you'll fall for anything.

Steve Bartkowski, NFL Quarterback

September 4

The Lord will guide you always; he will satisfy your

needs in a sun-scorched land.... You will be like

a well-watered garden, like a spring

whose waters never fail.

ISAIAH 58:11 NIV

April 29

If it doesn't matter if you win or lose, but how you play
the game, why do we keep score?

CHARLEY BOSWELL, BLIND PROFESSIONAL GOLFER

September 3

You find that you have peace of mind and can enjoy yourself, get more sleep, and rest when you know that it was a 100 percent effort that you gave, win or lose.

GORDIE HOWE, NHL CENTER, RIGHT WING, DEFENSE

April 30

I can believe I won, but what I can't believe or get over

is why God has blessed me so much.

PENNY HEYNS, SWIMMER, OLYMPIC GOLD MEDALIST

September 2

God, there is nothing I have ever done to deserve

how much You love me.

BRYAN JENNINGS, SURFING CHAMPION

May 1

May the God who gives endurance and

encouragement give you a spirit of

unity among yourselves.

ROMANS 15:5 NIV

September 1

Perhaps the single most important element in mastering the techniques and tactics of racing is experience. But once you have the fundamentals, acquiring the experience is a matter of time.

GREG LEMOND, CYCLIST, TOUR DE FRANCE WINNER

May 2

I've always tried to coach people the way I would like

to be coached: positively and encouragingly rather

than with criticism and fear.... I've tried to be

as fair as possible.

TONY DUNGY, NFL COACH

August 31

Basketball is just something else to do, another facet of life. I'm going to be a success at whatever I choose because of my preparation. By the time the game starts, the outcome is already decided. I never think about having a bad game, because I have prepared.

DAVID ROBINSON, NBA CENTER

May 3

People say that I'm the most competitive person they have ever seen. But it's my passion for the game that makes me this way. I believe that playing every game at breakneck speed is fun.

DON MATTINGLY, MAJOR LEAGUE FIRST BASEMAN

August 30

The Lord is my strength and my song; he has become

my salvation. Shouts of joy and victory resound

in the tents of the righteous.

PSALM 118:14-15 NIV

May 4

Kicking last-second "winning" field goals doesn't make me a champion, but putting God first in life can make anyone a winner.

DOUG PELFREY, NFL PLACE KICKER

August 29

There are four parts of self that lead to success.

The first part is discipline, the second is concentration,

the third is patience, and the fourth is faith.

GEORGE FOSTER, MAJOR LEAGUE OUTFIELDER

May 5

I've always made a total effort, even when the odds
seemed entirely against me. I never quit trying;
I never felt that I didn't have a chance to win.

ARNOLD PALMER, PROFESSIONAL GOLFER

August 28

If all I'm remembered for is being a good basketball player, then I've done a bad job with the rest of my life.

ISAIAH THOMAS, NBA GUARD

May 6

The Lord will fulfill his purpose for me;

your love, O Lord, endures forever.

PSALM 138:8 NIV

August 27

If Henry Ford hadn't kept going in the early days despite ridicule, we would never have seen the Ford car. It's been the same with every great man you could name. He kept plugging when everybody said his chances of making first base were nil.

You just can't beat the person who never gives up.

BABE RUTH, MAJOR LEAGUE PITCHER AND OUTFIELDER

May 7

I wouldn't be able to do what I'm doing without faith....
My running is a way I can express my faith, because there
are so many odds against me. I believe God gave me a
gift in being able to run, and I want to give back to Him
because He takes care of me and meets all my needs.

EVELYN ASHFORD, SPRINTER,
FOUR-TIME OLYMPIC GOLD MEDALIST

August 26

Somebody will always break your records.

It is how you live that counts.

EARL CAMPBELL, NFL Fullback

May 8

You can't get much done in life if you only work

on the days when you feel good.

JERRY WEST, NBA COACH

August 25

For this very reason, make every effort to add to your faith goodness; and to goodness, knowledge; and to knowledge, self-control; and to self-control, perseverance; and to perseverance, godliness; and to godliness, brotherly kindness; and to brotherly kindness, love.

2 PETER 1:5-7 NIV

May 9

It's never an upset if the so-called underdog has all

along considered itself the better team.

WOODY HAYES, COLLEGE FOOTBALL COACH

August 24

It's what you learn after you know it all that counts.

JOHN WOODEN,
COLLEGE BASKETBALL COACH

May 10

Whenever people talk about baseball, they don't say, "work ball," they say, "play ball." It should be fun.

WILLIE STARGELL, MAJOR LEAGUE FIRST BASEMAN

August 23

Most of all,

I want to be respected for being a godly man.

STEVE WALLACE, NFL TACKLE

May 11

The Lord says, "I will make my people strong
with power from me!... Wherever they go,
they will be under my personal care."

ZECHARIAH 10:12 TLB

August 22

Whether you're trying to excel in athletics or in any other field, always practice. Look, listen, learn—and practice, practice, practice. There is no substitute for work, no shortcut to the top.

FRANK ROBINSON, MAJOR LEAGUE OUTFIELDER

May 12

Golf is not a game of great shots.

It's a game of the least misses.

The people who win make the fewest mistakes.

GENE LITTLER, PROFESSIONAL GOLFER

August 21

Setting goals for your game is an art. The trick is in setting them at the right level—neither too low nor too high. A good goal should be lofty enough to inspire hard work, yet realistic enough to provide solid hope of attainment.

GREG NORMAN, PROFESSIONAL GOLFER

May 13

A̶ll I could think about was, "What am I going to do if I don't play baseball?" That's when I realized that baseball was my top priority in life. I no longer had control of the situation, and I had to trust God to work things out. I rearranged my priorities by placing God first, my family second, and baseball third.

BRIAN HARPER, MAJOR LEAGUE CATCHER

August 20

It takes wisdom to have a good family, and it takes

understanding to make it strong.

PROVERBS 24:3 NCV

May 14

I dribbled by the hour with my left hand when I was young. I didn't have full control, but I got so I could move the ball back and forth from one hand to the other without breaking the cadence of my dribble. I wasn't dribbling behind my back or setting up any trick stuff, but I was laying the groundwork for it.

BOB COUSY, NBA GUARD

August 19

To me, it was the path getting [to the Olympics] that counted, not the number of gold medals I won. My advice to young people is to relax, enjoy the journey, enjoy every moment, and quit worrying about winning or losing.

Matt Biondi, Swimmer,
Five-Time Olympic Gold Medalist

May 15

I used to look at people for how they could help me,

but now my perspective is how I can help them.

TRENT DILFER, NFL QUARTERBACK

August 18

The most important thing you have in your life is your faith, and it will help you through many trials and tribulations.

GERRY FAUST, COLLEGE FOOTBALL COACH

May 16

Be strong in the Lord and in his mighty power. Put on the full armor of God so that you can take your stand.

EPHESIANS 6:10-11 NIV

August 17

Really, it comes down to your philosophy.

Do you want to be safe and good, or do you

want to take a chance and be great?

JIMMY JOHNSON, NFL COACH

May 17

Do you believe you're a starter or a benchwarmer?
Do you believe you're an all-star or an also-ran? If the
answers to these questions are the latter, your play on the
field will reflect it. But when you've learned to...believe in
yourself, there's no telling how good a player you can be.
That's because you have the mental edge.

ROD CAREW, MAJOR LEAGUE FIRST AND
SECOND BASEMAN, DESIGNATED HITTER

August 16

When time is running out and the score is close,
most players are thinking, I don't want to be the
one to lose the game, but I'm thinking,
What do I have to do to win?

JERRY WEST, NBA GUARD

May 18

Do you know what my favorite part of the game is?

The opportunity to play. It's as simple as that.

MIKE SINGLETARY, NFL LINEBACKER

August 15

In quietness and trust is your strength....

The Lord longs to be gracious to you;

he rises to show you compassion.

ISAIAH 30:15,18 NIV

May 19

You miss 100 percent of the shots you never take.

WAYNE GRETZKY, NHL CENTER

August 14

I look to the Lord seeking guidance for my life...the
bottom line is, the Lord has the answers.

DOUG HENRY, MAJOR LEAGUE PITCHER

May 20

You must have a dream for your future. Remember
that if you allow God to be a partner in your life,
He will help you with all your dreams. But remember,
the Lord expects your cooperation. You must be willing
to give of yourself totally, that is, spiritually, mentally,
emotionally, and physically.

BUCKY DENT, MAJOR LEAGUE SHORTSTOP

August 13

I judge a person's worth by the kind of person he is in life—by the way he treats his fellow man, by the way he wants to be treated, and by the way he respects people around him.

CALVIN MURPHY, NBA GUARD

May 21

May they who love you be like the sun

when it rises in its strength.

JUDGES 5:31 NIV

August 12

Hard work always pays off. If you really have a lot of interest in learning, you'll do well.

EDGAR MARTINEZ, MAJOR LEAGUE THIRD BASEMAN

May 22

I never think about missing a free throw. All that goes through my mind when I'm at the free throw line is seeing the ball go through the bottom of the net.

BRAD DAUGHERTY, NBA CENTER

August 11

The knowledge that my life is in God's hands helps me
to keep my composure or regain it in tough situations.

TOM LANDRY, NFL COACH

May 23

I don't pay attention to what others are doing.
I feel strongly that if I have correct goals and the
determination to keep pursuing them the best way
I know how, everything else falls into line.

DAN DIERDORF, NFL OFFENSIVE TACKLE

August 10

Blessed is the man who perseveres under trial, because
when he has stood the test, he will receive the crown of
life that God has promised to those who love him.

JAMES 1:12 NIV

May 24

I don't play small. You have to go out and play with
what you have. I admit I used to want to be tall.
But I made it in high school, college, and now the pros.
So it doesn't matter.

SPUD WEBB, 5'7" NBA GUARD

August 9

If your work is not fired with enthusiasm, you will be
fired with enthusiasm.

JOHN MAZUR, NFL COACH

May 25

I hope that I epitomize the American Dream. For I came against long odds, from the ghetto to the very top of my profession. I was not immediately good at basketball. It did not come easy. It came as a result of a lot of hard work and self-sacrifice.

BILL RUSSELL, NBA CENTER

August 8

If you stay in the Word of God,

you can overcome anything.

BRIAN SKINNER, NBA CENTER

May 26

Blessed are those who dwell in your house;

they are ever praising you. Blessed are those

whose strength is in you.

PSALM 84:4-5 NIV

August 7

Friendships born on the field of athletic strife are the real gold of competition. Awards become corroded, friends gather no dust.

JESSE OWENS, SPRINTER,
FOUR-TIME OLYMPIC GOLD MEDALIST

May 27

God has given me opportunities, given me skills, and my job is to do the best I can with those skills and let the results fall where God allows.

TONY DUNGY, NFL COACH

August 6

Achieving success and personal glory in athletics has less to do with wins and losses than it does with learning how to prepare yourself so that at the end of the day, whether on the track or in the office, you know that there was nothing more you could have done to reach your ultimate goal.

JACKIE JOYNER-KERSEE, TRACK AND FIELD, THREE-TIME OLYMPIC GOLD MEDALIST

May 28

We need to know where we are going and how we plan to get there. Our dreams and aspirations must be translated into real and tangible goals with priorities and time frames.

MERLIN OLSEN, NFL TACKLE

August 5

I have learned to be content, whatever the circumstances may be. I know now how to live when things are difficult and I know how to live when things are prosperous.... I am ready for anything through the strength of the One who lives within me.

PHILIPPIANS 4:11-13 PHILLIPS

May 29

Whenever two teams or players of equal ability play,

the one with the greater courage will win.

PETE CARRIL, COLLEGE BASKETBALL COACH

August 4

I've never lost a game in my life.

Once in a while, time ran out on me.

BOBBY LAYNE, NFL QUARTERBACK

May 30

Class is honesty. Honesty with yourself makes you

comfortable with yourself. It also makes you

understand that you're no better or worse

than anyone else.

KATHY WHITWORTH, PROFESSIONAL GOLFER

August 3

The presence of a living God and His unconditional

love...set the stage for my athletic success because I

then knew I could risk failure. My identity would not

be based on whether I won or lost.

KYLE ROTE, JR., PROFESSIONAL SOCCER PLAYER

May 31

I can do everything through him

who gives me strength.

PHILIPPIANS 4:13 NIV

August 2

You can't measure success if you have never failed.
My father has taught me that if you really do want to
reach your goals, you can't spend any time worrying
about whether you're going to win or lose.

Focus only on getting better.

STEFFI GRAF, PROFESSIONAL TENNIS PLAYER

June 1

When I was coaching, the one thought that I would try to get across to my players was that in everything I do each day, in everything I say, I must think first of what effect it will have on everyone concerned.

FRANK LAYDEN, NBA COACH

August 1

I probably have a different mental approach to swimming than most people. I actually enjoy training.

DAWN FRASER, SWIMMER,
THREE-TIME OLYMPIC GOLD MEDALIST

June 2

When things get tough, we like to refer to a little piece of paper that Dusty Baker carries in his pocket.... It's from Romans 5:1-5: "Tribulations bring about perseverance, and perseverance brings about proven character, and proven character brings about hope, and hope does not disappoint."

TOMMY LASORDA, MAJOR LEAGUE MANAGER

July 31

"For I know the plans I have for you," declares the Lord, "plans to prosper you and not to harm you, plans to give you hope and a future."

JEREMIAH 29:11 NIV

June 3

It is one of the strange ironies of this strange life that those who work the hardest, who subject themselves to the strictest discipline, who give up certain pleasurable things in order to achieve a goal, are the happiest.

BRUTUS HAMILTON, TRACK TEAM COACH,
1952 HELSINKI OLYMPICS

July 30

I have had some tough times.... Just because you have faith and believe in God doesn't mean you're perfect. But I have that comfort. I know there is someone higher to protect me.

MARY JOE FERNANDEZ, PROFESSIONAL TENNIS PLAYER

June 4

I feel it's important to bounce back after a bad performance. The sooner you get back out there, the better you feel inside. The only people who are failures are those who give up and don't continue fighting. Look at it this way: How would we be able to judge success if we didn't experience failure?

DAN MARINO, NFL QUARTERBACK

July 29

Winning takes character. Workers get the most out of themselves. When a body has a limited talent, it must muster all its resources of character to overcome adversity.

<small>PETE CARRIL, COLLEGE BASKETBALL COACH</small>

June 5

The Sovereign Lord is my strength;

he makes my feet like the feet of a deer,

he enables me to go on the heights.

HABAKKUK 3:19 NIV

July 28

Show me a guy who's afraid to look bad,

and I'll show you a guy you can beat every time.

LOU BROCK,
MAJOR LEAGUE OUTFIELDER

June 6

God is my rock. He is the stability of my life.

JENNIFER AZZI, WNBA GUARD

July 27

Any time you try to win everything, you must be

willing to lose everything.

LARRY CSONKA, NFL FULLBACK

June 7

Some clubs want to win so much they'll do anything to get it. Our approach has been just the opposite. We've tried to do things the right way. And the right way is [abiding by] the rules and regulations.... I may not like all of them, but once they are [official], we play by them.

DON SHULA, NFL COACH

July 26

We...pray that you will be strengthened with his glorious power so that you will have all the patience and endurance you need. May you be filled with joy, always thanking the Father, who has enabled you to share the inheritance that belongs to God's holy people, who live in the light.

COLOSSIANS 1:11-12 NLT

June 8

The true warrior understands and seizes that moment by giving an effort so intense and so intuitive that it could only be called one from the heart.

PAT RILEY, NBA PLAYER AND COACH

July 25

We have to remember that when life is hard,

God is there for us.

CHAD HENNINGS, NFL DEFENSIVE TACKLE

June 9

Nothing good comes in life or athletics unless a lot of hard work has preceded the effort. Only temporary success is achieved by taking shortcuts.

ROGER STAUBACH, NFL QUARTERBACK

July 24

My mother taught me very early to believe

I could achieve any accomplishment I wanted to.

The first was to walk without braces.

WILMA RUDOLPH, SPRINTER,
THREE-TIME OLYMPIC GOLD MEDALIST

June 10

May the God of peace himself make you entirely pure and devoted to God; and may your spirit and soul and body be kept strong.

1 THESSALONIANS 5:23 TLB

July 23

I feel that the most important step in any major accomplishment is setting a specific goal. This enables you to keep your mind focused on your goal and off the many obstacles that will arise while you're striving to do your best.

KURT THOMAS, GYMNAST, OLYMPIC GOLD MEDALIST

June 11

I don't step into a race car without asking the Lord
to put His angels around it.

KYLE PETTY, RACE CAR DRIVER

July 22

I'd rather have preparation than motivation.

Everyone likes to play, but no one likes to practice.

BUM PHILLIPS, NFL COACH

June 12

A winner is one who is not afraid of the challenge,

who rebounds from his setbacks, and who is flexible

enough to make adjustments in order to

· succeed the next time.

DAVE WINFIELD, MAJOR LEAGUE OUTFIELDER

July 21

Let us hold unswervingly to the hope we profess,

for he who promised is faithful. And let us consider how

we may spur one another on toward

love and good deeds.

HEBREWS 10:23-24 NIV

June 13

The man who can drive himself further once the effort

gets painful is the man who will win.

ROGER BANNISTER, RUNNER,
FIRST UNDER-FOUR-MINUTE MILER

July 20

I don't think I can play any other way but all out....

I enjoy the game so much because

I'm putting so much into it.

GEORGE BRETT, MAJOR LEAGUE THIRD BASEMAN

June 14

Some people are so busy learning the tricks of the trade

that they never learn the trade.

VERNON LAW, MAJOR LEAGUE PITCHER

July 19

You're always going to face criticism, you're always
going to face challenges, but those things are there
to make you stronger and more committed to
what God gives you.

DAVID ROBINSON, NBA CENTER

June 15

Everyone who competes in the games goes into strict training. They do it to get a crown that will not last; but we do it to get a crown that will last forever. Therefore I do not run like a man running aimlessly; I do not fight like a man beating the air. No, I beat my body and make it my slave so that after I have preached to others, I myself will not be disqualified for the prize.

1 CORINTHIANS 9:25-27 NIV

July 18

I learned that the only way to get anywhere in life is to work hard at it. Whether you're a musician, a writer, an athlete, or a businessman, there is no getting around it.

If you do, you'll win—if you don't, you won't.

BRUCE JENNER, DECATHLETE, OLYMPIC GOLD MEDALIST

June 16

Anyone can support a team that's winning—it doesn't take courage. But to stand behind a team, to defend a team when it is down and really needs you, that takes a lot of courage.

BART STARR, NFL QUARTERBACK

July 17

The man who complains about the way the ball

bounces is likely the one who dropped it.

LOU HOLTZ, COLLEGE FOOTBALL COACH

June 17

You have to have faith in God and faith in yourself

if you want others to have faith in you.

RON TURCOTTE, PROFESSIONAL JOCKEY

July 16

We throw open our doors to God and discover at the same moment that he has already thrown open his door to us. We find ourselves standing where we always hoped we might stand—out in the wide open spaces of God's grace and glory, standing tall and shouting our praise.

ROMANS 5:2 THE MESSAGE

June 18

People who enjoy what they do, invariably

do it well.

JOE GIBBS, NFL COACH

July 15

Enthusiasm is everything.

It must be as taut and vibrating as a guitar string.

PELÉ, PROFESSIONAL SOCCER PLAYER

June 19

Remember, "Rome was not built in a day." Instant success is never possible. Competence results only from sustained, consistent, self-disciplined effort over an extended period of time.

BUD WILKINSON, NFL COACH

July 14

I need to take basketball seriously to a certain point,

but at one point realize this is all background music.

The most important thing is to do right and please God.

RUTHIE BOLTON, WNBA GUARD

June 20

I will teach you wisdom's ways and lead you in straight paths. If you live a life guided by wisdom, you won't limp or stumble as you run. Carry out my instructions; don't forsake them. Guard them, for they will lead you to a fulfilled life.

PROVERBS 4:11-13 NLT

July 13

Negative thoughts are contagious and they get passed around like a disease. I try to inoculate myself against the fear of failure.

BILL FOSTER, COLLEGE BASKETBALL COACH

June 21

I believe there is a price tag on everything worthwhile, but it is seldom a monetary one. The price is more often one of dedication, deprivation, extra effort, loneliness. Each person decides whether he or she wants to pay the price. Those who do, achieve beyond other people.

JIM MCKAY, SPORTS BROADCASTER

July 12

I'll never worry about not being successful. I'll just take

it one day at a time, one season at a time.

And play as hard as I can.

BO JACKSON,
NFL RUNNING BACK AND MAJOR LEAGUE OUTFIELDER

June 22

If I work on a certain move constantly, finally it doesn't seem so risky to me. The idea is that the move stays dangerous and it looks dangerous to my foes, but not to me. Hard work has made it easy. That is my secret. That is why I win.

NADIA COMANECI, GYMNAST,
FIVE-TIME OLYMPIC GOLD MEDALIST

July 11

May...God our Father, who loved us and by his grace

gave us eternal encouragement and good hope,

encourage your hearts and strengthen you in every good

deed and word.

2 Thessalonians 2:16-17 NIV

June 23

My relationship with Jesus has become

my number one priority.

JON KITNA, NFL QUARTERBACK

July 10

Having fun is the name of the game. We all go out there and play as hard as we can to try to win. But the main reason we play is to have fun. Never do anything you don't enjoy. I've always said that when I stop having fun, I'll leave the game.

JOE CARTER, MAJOR LEAGUE OUTFIELDER

June 24

I just love the game of basketball so much. The game! I don't need the 18,000 people screaming and all the peripheral things. To me, the most enjoyable part is the practice and preparation.

BOBBY KNIGHT, COLLEGE BASKETBALL COACH

July 9

My focus has gradually changed from pleasing myself

to pleasing God.

TRENT DILFER, NFL QUARTERBACK

June 25

Love the Lord your God with all your heart

and with all your soul and with all your mind

and with all your strength.

MARK 12:30 NIV

July 8

Grasping your capabilities allows you to work within

your limits and to achieve emotional, spiritual,

and physical excellence within your realm.

No one needs to be like someone else.

DENNIS POTVIN, NHL DEFENSEMAN

June 26

I was determined to play. I knew all along deep down inside that I could do it, that I was good even though hardly anyone seemed to agree with me. My determination more than made up for any lack of speed, height, or weight.

JACK LAMBERT, NFL LINEBACKER

July 7

You can't be a good leader without good character.

TONY BOSELLI, NFL OFFENSIVE TACKLE

June 27

If you want to hit .300, set your sights on .325. If you want to drive in 100 runs, go for 125. Then, if you fall a little short and hit .304 and drive 100 runs, you won't be disappointed.

KEN SINGLETON, MAJOR LEAGUE OUTFIELDER

July 6

So, chosen by God for this new life of love, dress

in the wardrobe God picked out for you: compassion,

kindness, humility, quiet strength, discipline.

COLOSSIANS 3:12 THE MESSAGE

June 28

I realized early that I may never become adept at controlling the ball with my feet. Therefore, I will have to make up for it in other ways such as speed, willingness to make contact, the ability to leap into the air, and hustle.

KYLE ROTE, JR., PROFESSIONAL SOCCER PLAYER

July 5

I am willing to put myself through anything; temporary pain or discomfort means nothing to me as long as I can see that the experience will take me to a new level. I am interested in the unknown, and the only path to the unknown is through breaking barriers, an often painful process.

DIANA NYAD, LONG-DISTANCE SWIMMER, FIRST PERSON TO SWIM FROM THE BAHAMAS TO THE US

June 29

I have a basic philosophy that I've tried to follow during my coaching career. Whether you're winning or losing, it is important to always be yourself. You can't change because of the circumstances around you.

COTTON FITZSIMMONS, NBA COACH

July 4

The price of success is hard work, dedication to the job at hand, and the determination that whether we win or lose, we have applied the best of ourselves to the task at hand.

VINCENT T. LOMBARDI, NFL COACH

June 30

O Lord, you alone are my hope.... My success—at which so many stand amazed—is because you are my mighty protector. All day long I'll praise and honor you, O God, for all that you have done for me.

PSALM 71:5-8 TLB

July 3

Every day I didn't get a hit, my confidence sank lower.

It was starting to get to me.... I was trying so many

different stances, taking everybody's advice, and getting

confused. I finally realized that I had to go back

to what I did to get here.

CAL RIPKEN, JR., MAJOR LEAGUE THIRD BASEMAN

July 1

Over and over, it has been made crystal clear to me that the basics of life are important—love of God, family, and friends; a commitment to integrity so that you will be respected and respect yourself; and a commitment to leadership so that others will respect you because of your own actions.

MONTE CLARK, NFL COACH

July 2